AF506129

**MAJOR LEAGUE
BASEBALL
PLAYERS GUIDES**

How to Hit
and
Run the Bases

Hank Aaron
Felipe Alou
Johnny Bench
Rod Carew
Roberto Clemente
Donn Clendenon
Frank Howard
Alex Johnson
Harmon Killebrew
Willie Mays
Willie McCovey
Tony Oliva
Tony Perez
Boog Powell
Maury Wills

GROSSET & DUNLAP A NATIONAL GENERAL COMPANY

Publishers   *New York*

Contents

Hitting

SOME NON-BASEBALL player once wrote that the basic ingredient of hitting is *fear*—fear of being struck by the ball—and that a baseball player hits the ball in self-defense. Nothing could be more opposite to the truth. If a man goes to bat in a baseball game with the least trace of fear in his heart, he is already half struck out. For a timid batter, whose concern is to defend himself, is at the mercy of the pitcher.

What a hitter needs more than anything else is *confidence*. You must go up to the plate in an *aggressive* mood, feeling sure that you can sock the ball into fair territory, and relaxed enough to hold your ground against any pitcher long enough to make him throw you the pitch you like.

Of course it takes time—and lots of hitting—to develop that confidence. Hitting a pitched baseball is about as hard a task as any sport presents—harder than catching a forward pass in football, harder than tossing a basketball into the net, harder than placing a tennis ball or a golf ball where you want it to be. So it takes a great deal more practice than any of those other skills. To become a hitter you have to grab every chance you can to hit a pitched baseball. Hit it with anything. If you can't get a regular bat, hit it with a broomstick. If you can't get a regulation baseball, hit a tennis ball, or one of those plastic "whiffle" balls, or any sort of ball another fellow can throw to you.

Don't start out trying to set yourself in a "perfect" stance, with an ideal bat. Watch the guys on TV or at the ballpark and pick out a player whose build seems more like your own, or whose style of play is a style that suits you. Then imitate his stance and swing. If that does not suit you, watch another guy and imitate him. But *keep hitting!*

The Stance

Some teachers of hitting will tell you to find a stance in which you are comfortable and then stick to it and let nobody change it. We don't agree with that. When you are young, you should be ready to change your ways at the plate whenever you see another style that appeals to you. Eventually you'll find the style that gives you the best results and on that you can build your confidence. Also, you should listen to what anybody has to tell you about hitting. Never mind if he is thirty years out of the game. There may be some little thing he can offer that will suit *you*. So avoid that wise-guy "Who are you to tell me anything?" attitude. You'll be surprised where you can pick up little helpful hints. Of course you'll get a lot of lousy advice mixed in with the few valuable bits. But don't scorn any of it. As one old-timer used to advise: "Let it go in one ear. Hold it for a while. If it does not make sense after a few weeks, let it trickle out the other."

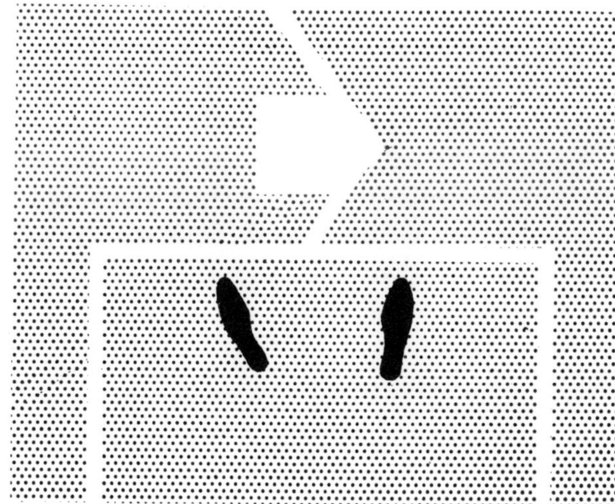

Parallel stance.

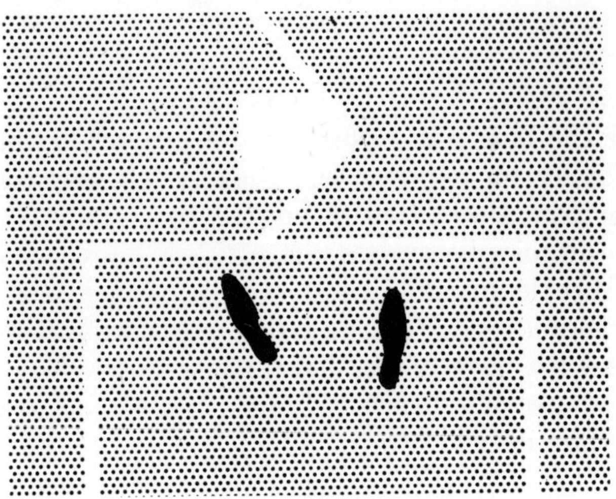

Closed stance.

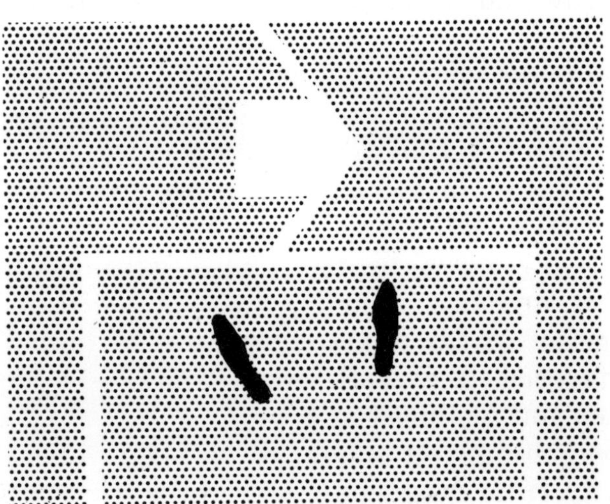

Open stance.

4

As for the bat, when you are still growing, you will probably be using a bat that is too big and heavy for you. Don't let this bother you. That happened to almost every one of us. You know even Mickey Mantle started practicing his hitting when he could not even lift a full-size bat and had to have one with part of the barrel sawed off. So go ahead and use big brother's bat if that's all you can get. The extra weight will help develop your muscles.

But don't use a bat so heavy you can't swing it and hit with it. The idea is to *hit*, to build confidence, and to train your muscles to respond automatically. So pick up something to hit. Get someone to throw you fast pitches. And hit and hit and hit.

As you make your start there are a few fundamentals you ought to keep in mind. One is your position with relation to the plate. You are required to stand inside a batter's box when you play regulation ball, so get in the habit of remaining relatively close to the plate—within bat's reach of it, anyway. Whether you stand with feet close together or far apart is a matter of individual preference. Try both ways and see which one makes you feel most at ease.

But one thing you should do is keep your elbows away from your body. If you don't do that, you will not get a full free swing at the ball. A batting swing should be smooth and loose, so that the bat will go right "through" the ball and continue on around your body. You can't swing that way if you keep your elbows tight against your ribs. So lift them up, away from your sides and *hold* them there as you await the pitch.

There is one part of a batting swing that some coaches never mention. That is the grip on the bat. While every coach will show you how to grab the handle of the bat, with the strong hand on the top, not many will remind you of the importance of a tight grip. You have to *squeeze* the bat handle if you are going to transfer the full strength

Stand within at least bat's reach of the plate.

6

of the blow from legs, back, shoulders, forearms, and wrists through the bat to the ball. If you hold the bat loosely, the force of the pitch will loosen it further and take much of the steam out of your swing. Notice how the good hitters keep tightening their hands on the bat handle. Sometimes it

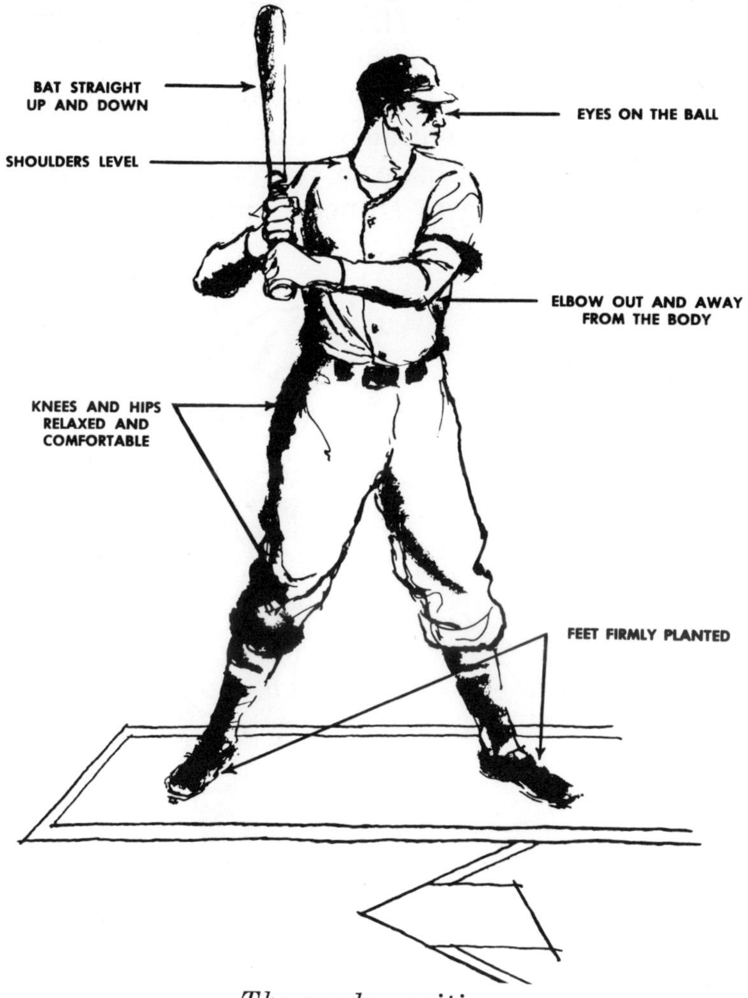

The ready position.

looks as if they are trying to wring some juice out of the wood, they tighten their fingers so. A strong pair of hands, therefore, is a necessary part of your equipment and when you are not able to swing a bat you can still get a sort of workout by exercising your grip.

Most good batters learn to "cock" the bat in some way before the pitch comes down. This, by getting the bat into hitting position beforehand, saves time on the swing and gives you that extra split second to size up the pitch as it approaches you. When the wrists are "cocked" they are held relatively high, almost shoulder height, and the bat will point straight up. But not all batters start their swing in this manner. Some will stand relaxed and cock the bat quickly, as they draw back their hands and arms, and twist their hips away from the pitcher, as if they were tightening a bowstring or pulling back the rubber on a slingshot. Whatever way you do it, you have to remember that the *first* part of the swing is this drawing back and tightening of the muscles, the coiling of the spring.

Of course, as you are making ready to hit, you *must* keep your eye on the ball. Lots of young batters neglect this very elemental part of the job, thinking it will be time enough to watch the ball when it is on the way. But keeping your eye on the ball means a great deal more than that. It means keeping the ball in sight every second, from the moment the pitcher takes his position on the mound. You will notice that the pitcher understands how important it is to you to keep that ball in sight, because he will do his best to keep you from seeing it. He will hold it behind his leg when he takes the sign, and keep it covered with his glove through part of his windup. But you must keep watching it, even if you see only a tiny slice of it, all the time. Watch it all the way to the bat. Watch it, if you can, to see what part of the bat you hit it with. If you take the pitch, then watch it right on past you to the catcher. As a matter of fact, it is good practice to stand at the plate and let pitches go by, while you watch them every second, right into the catcher's glove. In this way you can form a very valuable habit. You will also

The pitcher will do everything he can to hide the ball.

learn to keep your head from turning away from
the ball—a very bad habit indeed. Even some good
hitters sometimes forget to keep the head still and
will turn, as they swing, to see where the ball is
going to land. Too often when you do that, it lands
in the catcher's glove, because when you moved
your head you lost track of it and missed it by a
few inches.

The Grip

Your manner of holding your bat—whether
you take it at the end or choke up on it a few
inches—will probably change as you develop your
size and strength. Probably the best method, in
the beginning, is to choke up on the bat, placing
the hands a couple of inches above the knob. This

Choke grip.

will provide better control of the bat, just as a short grip on a hammer makes it easier to hit a nail on the head. It also will keep you from over-swinging, which is a very common fault with

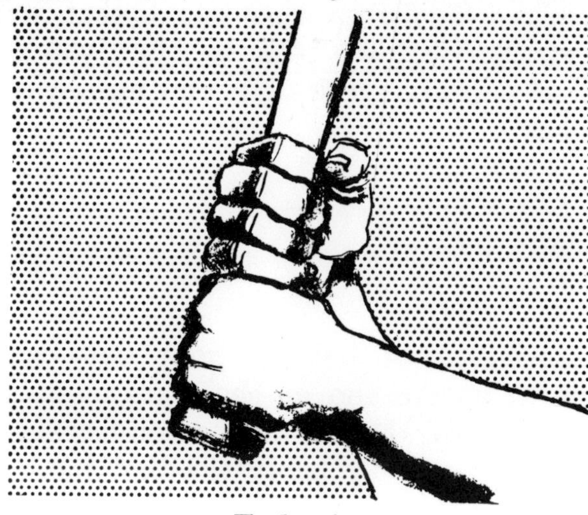

End grip.

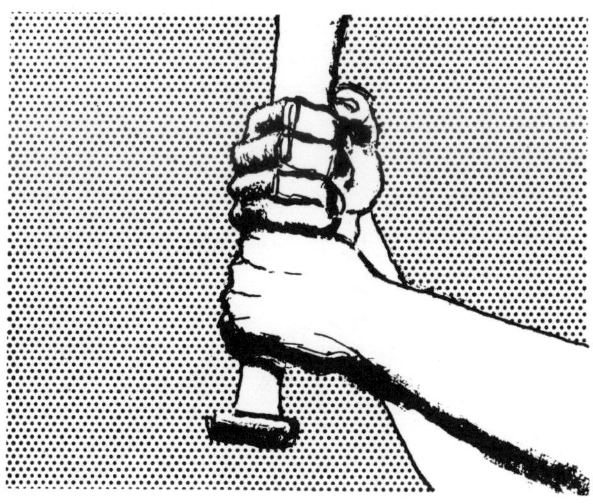

Modified grip.

many aspiring hitters. If you start swinging for the fences right from the start, you are going to develop a lot of bad habits. So concentrate on hitting the ball, with the bat always well under control. Eventually, if you are tall and strong, or just unusually well developed in shoulders and chest, you may hold the bat at the end and hit for distance.

The Hips

The need for confidence—for a complete lack of fear—is best shown in the way a batter uses his hips. A cautious batter, one who is thinking of bailing out of the box as soon as he sees a pitch that may hit him, will keep his hips—that is, his tail—sticking well out behind him, so that his weight will be already partly out of the box. But if you do not involve your hips in the swing, then a good part of your bodily strength will be canceled out and you will be merely pecking at the baseball.

In preparing to hit, you will notice many hitters give a little hip wiggle. Ted Williams was famous for this. What he was doing was getting his hips locked firmly into place, like the pivot of a wheel, so that the shove of his hind leg would be transmitted up through his body to combine with the striking power of shoulders, forearms, and wrists. When you practice your swing, you can actually feel the advantage of keeping your hips involved, for if they are off-center, sticking out behind you, the leg-thrust will follow a crooked path on the way up through your frame and most of it will be lost along the way.

This does not mean, of course, that you cannot crouch at the plate, as so many batters do in order to provide the pitcher with a smaller strike zone. (The umpire judges your strike zone according to

The confident batter turns his hip to the pitcher.

how you *normally* stand at the plate and if you normally crouch the distance between armpits and knees will of course be lessened.) But when you swing, you bring your hips back into line just before you step into the pitch.

You step into the pitch in order to meet it when you can apply maximum power. If you will try hitting a stationary object—even a ball hanging on a string or balanced on a post—you will observe that if you hit the ball when it is behind your body, you cannot apply all the strength your recoil has packed into your muscles. There arc many times when you may want to hit a ball "late" this way, for a specific purpose. But it is not the way to hit it full force.

The Stride

Of course, stepping into a pitch can mean a stride forward, or just a shifting of weight from the rear foot to the front foot, depending on whether you stand with your feet close together, with a wide spread, or with a modified spread. If you are most comfortable and confident and can hit most successfully with your feet close together, then you may step forward a full stride as you swing. But if you adjust best to the spreadlegged stance you may do no more than slide your forward foot an inch ahead, or not at all, just shifting the weight as you complete your swing. But whatever you do, you should remember to move

14

forward, into the pitch. Otherwise you will hit the ball a kind of going-away punch that has no sting in it at all.

Timid batters often step away from the pitch, toward the baseline, as they swing, and if they hit the ball at all they will just dribble it on the ground or pop it foul. But you will see some good batters who adopt an "open" stance, with the forward foot off toward first base or third base (depending on whether the batter is left- or right-handed) rather than toward the pitcher's box. But if you watch their feet as they swing, you will notice that the forward foot comes back into line and steps *forward.* They use the open stance because they feel it gives them a better look at the inside pitches which they may have found bothersome in the more common stance.

A man who uses the open stance is more likely to "spray" his hits—that is, hit them to whatever field the pitch has put them closest to—outside pitches to the "opposite" field (right field for a right-handed batter) and inside pitches to the natural field, where a batter hits a ball if he pulls it. The closed stance is more to the liking of men who like to pull all their hits. But this is not always true, for hitting habits and skills depend too on the hitter's strength, the length of his arms, the quickness of his swing, the suppleness of his wrists.

The same thing can be said of the close-together stance and the spread. Keeping the feet close together with a long stride into the ball when the pitch comes would seem best suited to the guys who hit the long ball. But study big-league ball-players for a while and you will see that some of the real power hitters use the spread stance, with almost no forward stride, and some of the spray hitters stand with the feet close together and take a full stride into the pitch. This then is largely a matter of what stance makes you feel most comfortable and confident. If a long stride causes you to take your eye off the ball for an instant, then try the spread stance. Or try the modified spread, with a relatively shorter stride. Just remember that no matter how you stand, the first move in your swing is the *recoil*—the drawing of the bowstring—in which you shift your weight to your rear foot and draw the bat back to get the snap and strength into your swing.

The cocking of the wrists is what gives the final snap to your batting swing, as it does to the blow you deal with a hammer. Try hitting a nail sometime with a hammer, without cocking your wrist. That is, lift the hammer as if your wrist were strapped tight so you could not bend it. Then try to drive a nail. You will get no strength at all into your blow. Likewise if you try to hit a baseball with a bat with no wrist action.

Some batters cock their wrists as they await the pitch, and others do it as part of the recoil action. You do what works best. If you have good fast reflexes, you can cock your wrists as you recoil. If you find you are late in getting your bat on the ball, you may want to save a split second by bending your wrists beforehand.

As a pitcher shoves himself off the rubber to put

his whole body into his pitch, so a hitter must push off his rear foot to get all his available strength. This is the reason you see a batter as he takes his stance begin to "dig in" with the toe of his rear foot. He does not want his foot to slip and deprive him of the good *shove* with which he shifts his weight from the rear foot to the front. Moving the rear foot as the pitch approaches is almost certain to reduce the power of your swing. (Of course there are times when you do not want to hit the ball with any power—when you are bunting to sacrifice for instance. Then you will move your rear foot right up and face the pitcher squarely.)

The Swing

A few coaches will tell you that the batting swing should always be level. Hit line drives, they tell you. And they teach you to get your wrists on a level with the pitch and swing with the bat parallel to the ground. But good pitchers will throw the ball most of the time in the lower half of the strike zone, between your belt and knees. How can you get your wrists down then to swing the bat in a level swing? It can't be done. The low pitch has to be handled with a swing that sees the fat part of the bat somewhat lower than the handle. Of course that means that the bat does not sweep through quite so wide a plane, and so there is less of an area in which the bat can meet the ball. That is why pitchers try to keep the ball down. And that is why there are relatively few batters who can hit the low pitch well.

When the ball comes in between the belt and armpits, that is when you are going to have the best chance of giving it a ride. And then you must take care to keep your bat level as you swing, and to swing all the way through the ball. On low pitch or high pitch, you must complete your swing with a good free follow-through that brings the bat right around your body.

But you will not always, and perhaps not often, turn your strength loose on a ball to ride it as far as you can. Indeed, if you are not powerfully built, and particularly if you are just getting started in the game, it is a mistake to try for the fences on every pitch. You will do best to follow the advice of the old-timers and hit the ball "not too hard and not too easy." Meet it squarely out in front of the plate with a good smooth stroke, sight right down the bat to see just where the ball and bat meet and you will hit safely more often and be of more value to your club.

If you find yourself striking out a lot, your best move is to take a shorter grip on your bat and to shorten your swing. You can see the value of this move, if you go back to the comparison to a hammer. Observe that you can control your aim with a hammer much better if you hold it part way up the handle, and if you do not swing the hammer through a long arc. That is, if you tap the nail instead of trying to lambaste it with your full strength, you have a chance of hitting it more often.

The fat part of the bat should be lower than the handle.

Likewise, as you try to improve your chances of hitting the ball, a short grip and a short swing give you better control. When you hit this way, the bat will not describe a full sweeping arc from one side of your body to the other. But you will still bring it *through* the ball as you complete the swing. You will not of course merely *tap* the ball. You will hit it smartly. Perhaps it will be like the difference between driving a spike and driving a finishing nail. With the spike, you use a heavy hammer that requires a mighty swing high over your head, each wallop trying to send the spike the whole distance. With a finishing nail you will not lift the hammer nearly so high. You will use a controlled blow, to send the nail in straight, a short distance at a time.

Even the mightiest of batters will often shorten their grip when they have two strikes, to increase their chances of meeting the ball with the bat. It is not a confession of weakness to choke the bat this way. It is a way of increasing the odds in your own favor.

Concentration

One aspect of batting in which many beginners fall short is *concentration*. They come to the plate with several matters on their minds. And while they *try* hard, they do not really center their minds intensely enough on the one job they are there for—to lay the bat on the ball. Concentration at the plate has got to be *fierce*. Of course you have to check over the position of the baserunners, if any, make sure you have all your signals straight, and know what the score is. But once you step in and fix your eye on the ball, you must never let your attention wander. Watch the ball with the ferocity of a snake getting ready to strike a bird. Watch it all the way down. See if you can make out the stitches!

As a matter of fact, practice in concentration and in keeping your eye on the ball ought to be what you do first. Stand at the plate in practice, at the start, and just watch that ball from pitcher's hand to catcher's hand, turning your head to see it hit the catcher's glove. When you know you can keep your eye on it *all the way*, then you are ready to try to hit it.

Bad Pitches

The next good habit to develop is the habit of leaving bad pitches alone. If you go after pitches that are out of your strike zone, you are increasing the odds in favor of the pitcher. Your strike zone is an oblong in the air, the width of the plate, and the height of the distance from your knees to your armpits. The pitcher is required to put the ball through that imaginary oblong. But if you habitually swing at pitches just beyond the plate, or just this side of the plate, or if you try to hammer at pitches just over your shoulders or below your knees, you are increasing the size of the pitcher's target.

Spend some time, therefore, in figuring out
what your strike zone looks like. Have someone
call the pitches for you and school yourself to
lay off the pitches that miss the zone. Above all,
never adopt the habit of "stopping" bad pitches
by reaching out to catch them on the bat. Forget
them! If they are not strikes, let them go. If you
get in the habit of reaching for bad pitches in
practice, you will sometimes do it in a game. So

The strike zone differs for every batter.

let those go. Concentrate with every last ounce of your attention on *all* the pitches, of course. But swing only at those that are going to be strikes.

Batting Practice

You will undoubtedly discover, after you have been hitting for a while, that there is a certain type of pitch that you miss more frequently. Perhaps an inside pitch ties you up. Perhaps a curve ball causes you to wave feebly as it sinks down and away. It might seem proper to put in all your time then in working on that particular pitch, having it thrown to you again and again until you find out how to hit it.

But that is not always such a good idea. The purpose of batting practice is to hit, and to build confidence through hitting. You want the batting practice pitcher to throw balls you can hit and you want to hit them and hit them, until you know you can do the job and enjoy doing it. Perhaps you will want to work on your stance and your swing as you hit. But most of all, you want to *hit*. When you have got your belly full of hitting, there will be time to work on your batting weakness. You may find that a different way of standing at the plate will enable you to hit the pitch you have been missing. Remember there have been great hitters in almost every stance known to man. Rogers Hornsby, one of the best who ever lived, used to stand in the rear outside corner of the batter's box—just as far away from the plate and from the pitcher as the rules permitted. Stan Musial used to turn himself into a corkscrew at the plate, twisting around so he seemed to be peeking at the pitcher over his shoulder. Babe Ruth held his feet close together, Joe DiMaggio and Ted Williams kept their feet well apart.

Sometimes opening the stance will enable you to handle the inside pitch better. But perhaps, to meet that pitch squarely, you need to recoil more before the pitch, instead of waiting until it is on the way. Then you may want to stand close to the plate, so that the only inside pitches that get by will be strikes, and go into a sort of crouch and twist that will get your wrists cocked well behind you and your arms pulled back about as far as they can go. Then you will be able to take an extra fraction of a second to size up the pitch and decide whether to go for it.

If you do find that a modified crouch is helpful, take care that in crouching you just do not stick your tail out behind you. Bend your knees and keep your tail in. If you merely lean over and stick your tail out, you will lose most of your leverage.

Most batters find that they do best by "hitting down" on the ball. That is, they keep the elbows high and bring the bat down sharply to get it on a level with the pitch. Actually, although you bring the bat down as you start your swing, you are not beating the ball downward, for the level bat, or the slightly dipped bat, if the pitch is low, should meet the ball squarely and send it back on a

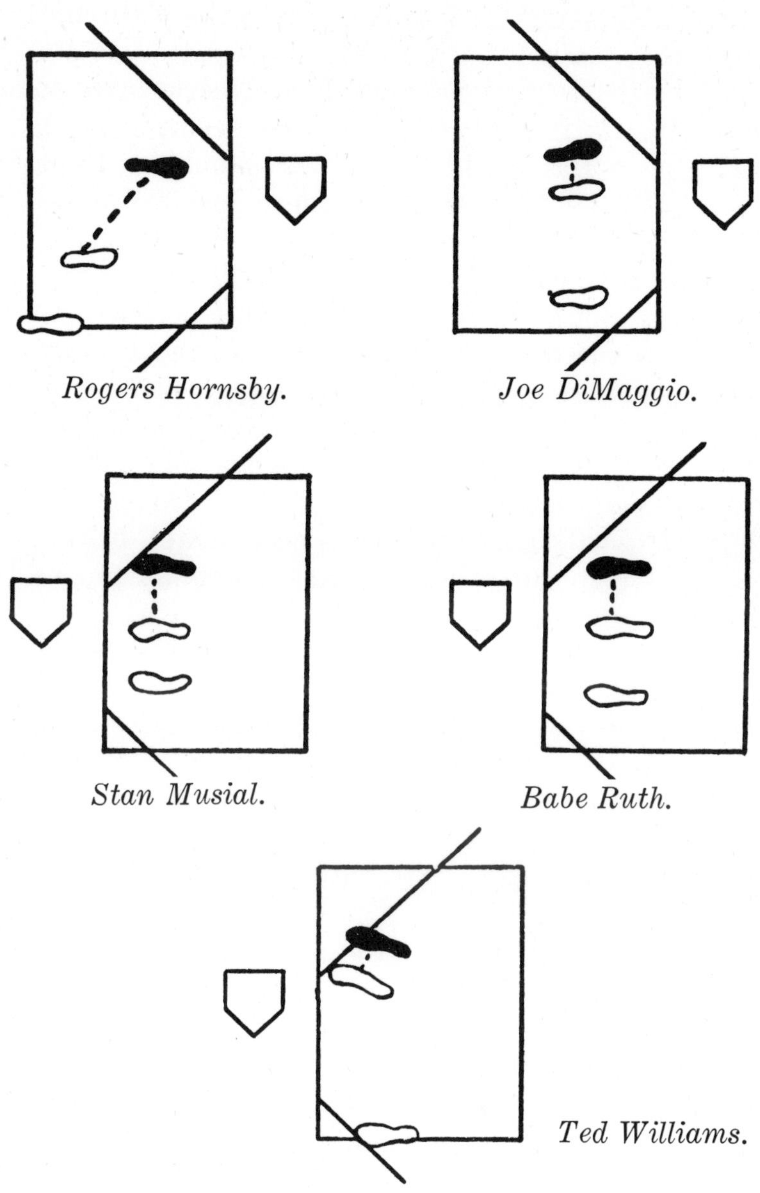

Stances of famous batters.

straight or rising flight. If you watch a good batting swing closely you will see that the bat does not sweep in a flat arc around the middle of the body. Instead it describes a sweeping arc, with the wrists starting above one shoulder and winding up above the other shoulder. That is why a good swing has a tendency to lift the ball, even uppercut it if the pitch is relatively low. But a conscious effort to hit the ball upward usually makes for a ragged swing, with a minimum of power. You can depend on the natural action of the bat to supply the lift that is needed. Just concentrate on meeting the ball squarely in front of the plate.

It should be obvious that no one can count on his natural instinct in developing a batting swing. It may seem "natural" to hold the bat loosely, to let it droop behind you as you await the pitch, or to hug it close to your body. But there are reasons why you should not do any of these things. If you hold the bat loosely, you will not transmit the power of your body directly to the bat. If you let the bat droop behind you it will have to be straightened up as you begin the swing, and this will mean a hitch of your motion and a waste of time. If you hug the bat to your body, you will be unable to swing it freely and so will not hit the ball with any snap at all.

While your stance and swing should be "comfortable" and "natural," they should first of all be calculated to do an efficient job of driving a pitched ball consistently into fair territory. That is why you need to experiment with them as you

develop your skill. You may be a much better
hitter than you think you are!

Summary

To sum up these basic points, then: Most batters will do best to learn bat control and not simply try to swing "from the tail" on every pitch
with all the strength of one's arms and body. Particularly when the count is two strikes, or when
it is especially vital to hit the ball safely, even the
strongest batter should be ready to shorten his
grip on the bat and shorten his swing in order to
increase his chances of laying the bat on the ball.

Elbows and arms should be kept away from the
body to enable you to swing quickly and freely.
The swing should begin with a recoil—and it may
be to your advantage to start this recoil before the
pitch approaches—that is, to incorporate part of
it into your stance. The wrists should be "cocked"
to insure full involvement of the arm muscles.

Above all, you should concentrate on the ball,
watching it from the moment the pitcher takes
it in his hand and keeping your eyes fixed on it,
sighting right down the bat at the ball, or watching it into the catcher's glove.

Bunting

THE ART OF bunting has been long neglected in major league baseball, even though a bunt is called for at some time in almost every game. Many players apparently take for granted that bunting is a simple act that requires neither study nor practice.

With the increasing use of artificial turf, however, there is bound to be increased attention to bunting. On the new surface, a bunt can skip along so quickly that it can get through the infield sometimes before a fielder can move over to cover it. And sacrifice bunts will have to be laid down with much greater care to keep them from turning into instant double plays.

The Sacrifice Bunt

Most sacrifice bunts that fail go wrong because the batter fails to flex his knees, because he does not get the bat at eye level, or because he jabs at the ball stiff-armed and so pops it up. The sacrifice bunt *is* a simple play but it does take practice. First of all, the batter should square around as soon as the pitcher starts to deliver the ball. He should bring his hind foot up beside his front foot and, standing at the front end of the box, face the pitcher directly. He should flex his knees, prepared to bend them deeply to get the bat down to meet a low pitch. The bat should be presented on a level, at right angles to the path of the pitch, as if you were holding it out for the pitcher to read the label. The hands can be well separated, one part way up the handle and one on the barrel of the bat, or both hands up on the barrel. The bat is gripped rather loosely, so it will give some with the pitch. The arms are extended toward the pitcher with elbows only slightly flexed at just about your own eye level so that you have a good

Square around for the sacrifice bunt.

sight at the approaching ball. The bat is not swung at the ball. Instead the ball is "caught" on the bat.

The bunt is directed by the angle of the bat, either to the right or left of the pitcher. If you catch the ball on the bat and do not jab at the ball, the ball should drop right on the ground and roll away from the plate, providing the time necessary for the runner to get from one base to the next.

Bunting to Get on Base

Bunting to get on base is an altogether different maneuver. First of all you do not betray your intention until the ball is on its way. A left-handed batter has the advantage in this department for he is a stride closer to first base. He bunts by "dragging" the ball, moving up toward the pitcher as the ball approaches, sliding one or both hands up on the bat, and tapping the ball with about the force used to drive a tack with a hammer. The important thing is that the left-handed batter moves *toward the pitcher*. He cannot leave the box before the ball is hit, although one foot may be out of the box. What he should *never* do is move toward the base before he has hit the ball, because then he will most likely miss the ball altogether. His first step, remember, is *forward*, toward the pitcher.

A right-handed batter does not drag a bunt because he must meet the ball square on before he starts across the plate for first base. He holds his regular stance at the plate, then swings the bat down suddenly by retracting his left hand and sliding his right hand up on the bat, so that the bat comes level, parallel to the ground and at right angles to the path of the ball. Then he taps the ball in whatever direction seems best. Usually a bunt down the third base line is most effective. It is harder for a catcher to handle, and it can be placed close enough to the line so the pitcher cannot reach it.

Just knowing how to hold the bat to bunt is of no value of course without practice. Pitchers especially should give plenty of time to bunting practice, because they are most frequently called on to sacrifice. But every batter can use a bunt to take advantage of a third baseman who is laying back too far, or "playing on his heels," or to help upset a pitcher or to haul himself out of a batting slump.

So practice bunting every day, for a set length of time, and keep at it until you learn exactly how to make the ball behave as it should. If you find yourself popping the bunts up, flex your elbows a bit and loosen your grip on the bat. If you miss

The bat is held loosely for the sacrifice bunt.

the low pitches or foul them, *bend your knees.* Squat right down to get the bat near eye level and level with the pitch. Expert bunters are going to be more and more valuable to their clubs as the use of artificial turf becomes more widespread.

The Butcher Boy

There is another batting maneuver that is not a bunt but that resembles a bunt because it is used often for the same purpose. This is the butcher-boy stroke or Baltimore chop. It is accomplished by suddenly shortening the grip on the bat—not in as exaggerated fashion as you do for the bunt but by sliding your hands up two or three inches from the knob of the bat so you have complete control—then chopping down on the ball as if you are trying to stun it as it goes by. The idea of course is to send the ball bouncing through the infield, to move a man from second to third or to bring a man in from third base. In amateur ball, where there are frequent throwing errors, it is sometimes a distinct advantage to get a batted ball on the ground in the infield to allow the fielders to start throwing the ball around. And this maneuver will undoubtedly become more popular with the increase of artificial turf, for a chopped ball may scoot through the "hole" between short and third about twice as fast as it might on ordinary turf.

Both these maneuvers, the bunt and the Baltimore chop, require confidence and complete control of the bat. They may not look so spectacular or bring as much applause as the long wallop into the seats or off the outfield fence. But they are often just about as valuable. And they are certainly better than a strike-out or a double-play. Baseball being a team game, it requires often that the batter forget his individual record and sacrifice a time at bat for the sake of moving a runner ahead.

When you perform a sacrifice, you are not charged with a time at bat. But there will be times when you will have to try to place your hit where you are very likely to be put out—and you will receive no credit for a sacrifice. The mighty hitter who is likely to break up a ball game with a long blow may not be required to do this often. But most ballplayers, even the ones with the .300 averages, have to be ready to forget their own averages and do what is going to help the club most. We can discuss this in greater detail when we talk of game situations.

Batter vs. Pitcher

THE BASIC CONTEST in every baseball game is between pitcher and batter. The point of the struggle may be expressed this way: The pitcher tries to make the batter hit *his* pitch; the batter tries to force the pitcher to throw him the batter's pitch.

The actual strategy works out to be an effort by the pitcher to get the batter into a spot where he must swing at whatever comes, while the batter tries to get the pitcher into a position where he *must* come in with a good pitch.

It should be clear enough then that if you go to the plate in a defensive mood, ready to swing at anything that comes near you, the pitcher already has the edge he wants. But if you approach the plate aggressively, convinced in your own mind that you can hit this pitcher whenever you want, you will be prepared to wait for the pitch you want. Above all you should not be afraid to let the pitcher get a strike on you. If his first pitch does not suit you, even if it is in the strike zone, you can let it go and *still* have plenty of time to get the sort of ball you are looking for.

When to Take a Pitch

When to take a pitch or when to swing are decisions that the coach sometimes flashes to you. But often you are on your own and you must use your head about whether you want to work the pitcher or start swinging. In general, the power pitcher, the man with the big motion and the sizzling fast ball, is the man who will suffer most if you make him throw extra pitches. Particularly if the day is hot, you may be able to get some of the zip off his fast ball by making him throw that extra pitch. But if the pitcher is a control pitcher, the

34

extra work will not bother him. In fact, he may even need to have you take a pitch or two so he can set you up for his best one, and if you hit the one you are not supposed to, especially when your club is behind, you may throw him off stride.

When to Lay Off

When you see a pitch you like there should be nothing tentative about your approach to it. You should not just beat it off, or make a pass at it. You should stride into it, attack it without hesitation, in order to do exactly what you want with it. It happens sometimes of course that just as you stride into the pitch you discover it is not what it seemed and you decide to lay off it. In that case, *lay off*. Pull back on your swing *hard* to keep your wrists from "breaking." (You will be surprised to discover that it takes real strength to pull back on a swing.) There is nothing more futile-looking than a batter who knows he has been fooled on a pitch still letting his swing be completed, half-heartedly, even with one hand, giving up a strike for no reason at all.

When you take a strike in order to get a look at what a pitcher is throwing, or to help time his speed, you are accomplishing something. But to swipe hopelessly at a pitch is to put yourself in a hole both psychologically and physically.

You will find a lot of people who will urge you not to try to "guess" with a pitcher, but to be ready to hit whatever comes your way that looks hittable. But you could spend a long long time in big league locker rooms looking for a man who did not guess with the pitcher. You might find a few liars who insisted they never did. But most hitters, no matter what they say, cannot help trying to figure what the pitcher may try to get him out with. It is just human nature to use your brain to make note of the kind of pitches they throw to you in different situations. It is true of course that when you rely too heavily on your guess you can be made to look pretty stupid, standing with your bat on your shoulder waiting for the ball to curve.

But if a pitcher has put you out with a low curve a couple of times, you know perfectly well that he is going to use that pitch the next time he has you in a hole—and you are really stupid if you don't look for it. Of course this guessing business sometimes becomes pretty refined, especially after you have faced a certain pitcher several times over a full season and he has come to know your habits and weaknesses as you have learned his. Then he may figure that you will be guessing "low curve" and he may decide suddenly to cross you up with a slider or some such thing. And if you have become too confident of your ability to guess with him, you will find yourself sud-

denly back on the bench. So take care that, as
you try to think with the pitcher, you do not grow
careless. You can *expect* a certain type of pitch.
But you must be *ready* for anything.

Studying the Opposition

Each pitcher has his own private method of delivering the ball, his own windup, his own arm-
style (overhand, sidearm, three-quarter, etc.) and
of course every pitcher is slightly different in
speed of delivery. It pays therefore to study pitchers all the time if you mean to be a successful batter. Occasionally you will even find a pitcher who
gives away his curve ball (by not raising his hands
quite so high as he begins his windup, by studying the ball in his glove as he makes it ready to
throw, by showing more or less seam on the ball
as he holds it while taking the sign) and you can
take advantage of this advance knowledge.

But even though you cannot discover the pitch
in advance, you can at least learn to time the
man's fast ball, observe just at what point in his
motion the ball is released, where he stands on
the rubber, and whether he has control of his
breaking pitches. Sometimes it is even possible to
time a man while he is taking his warm-up pitches.
You can stand away from the plate and swing
the bat as the ball reaches the plate, in this way
establishing the proper rhythm to meet his pitch
at the right time. But the best way to size up a

new pitcher is to stand at the plate and watch what he throws you. To do this you have to have the confidence to let him get a strike on you. And if he misses the strike zone on the first pitch, then you can look at two pitches.

You will soon learn that the opposition follows a general pattern in trying to get you out. It is to your advantage to make note of this pattern and remember it. There is one aspect of this, however, that you should always bear in mind—that is, that it is the catcher as much as the pitcher who sets the pattern. And because there are fewer catchers than there are pitchers, it is easier to keep track of the patterns the different catchers follow.

One guy may habitually call for a high inside pitch to be followed by a low outside curve. Another guy may rely on the slider in a pinch. Another guy may always call for the fast ball on three and two. And so on. Never fail to keep track of these things. Sometimes it may take a long time before you begin to discover just what the pattern is, but the study will be worth your while. You will find it far easier and often more profitable to learn catchers' habits than to learn pitchers'.

Correcting Your Weaknesses

Of course you can count on the fact that pitchers and catchers will be studying your habits too, will soon learn what sort of pitch you favor, what

you can't hit, whether you are likely to go for the
first ball, if you can be fooled by a change-up.
And so, as you gather more experience and more
confidence, you will be well repaid by working on
your batting weaknesses and overcoming them.
If you have been a sucker for a curve, you should
begin to study out ways of hitting curves safely.
Have someone throw them to you steadily day
after day and find out what you need to do—
lay back on them, shorten your grip and swing,
close your stance a little, stand closer to the plate,
or what. Eventually you will find out how to hit
them and then you will, for a while, enjoy a special advantage. That is, you will be getting curve
balls when the pitcher is in a tight spot, or when
he thinks he has you in one. And you will be able
to hit them.

A man who can be relied on to hit the ball
safely, or at least not to pop up or strike out, will
always find employment in baseball, even if his
other work is not outstanding. He may be counted
on especially as a pinch hitter and will find himself coming to bat often with men in scoring position. There are men in baseball who think that
coming up as a pinch hitter is like being placed
on a hotspot, where you must deliver—or *else*. But
if you stop and think about the situation, you will
realize this is not the fact at all. In such a situation, the psychological pressure, if there is any,
is on the *pitcher*. He is the one who is on the spot
and must come through or be in real trouble, for
usually there is a man or men in scoring position
and ordinarily he cannot afford to let you get

away. These circumstances give *you* the edge. You can afford to look the pitcher over, to wait for *your* pitch, to let him stew and fret a little and begin to tense up.

And you can remain aggressive—not trying to rap the first pitch you see but just fixing your eye on that baseball and waiting for it to come in where you can bust the heck out of it.

There will be of course certain types of pitches that will always be tough for you and some of them you may just have to school yourself to *avoid*. If you keep missing the high outside pitch for instance, you should train yourself to let it go by, except when there are two strikes and the pitch is close to the strike zone.

With two strikes on you, you cannot afford to wait any longer to see the exact pitch you like. So you have to adjust to be ready to get your bat on whatever comes close to being a strike. Unless you are the sharpest-eyed character in the country, do not count on being able to tell when a pitch is going to miss the strike zone by an inch or two. If it *looks* like a possible strike, don't let it get by. Above all, don't trust the umpire to agree with you that the pitch is just out of the strike zone. Umpires sometimes have different ideas about what is and is not a strike. With two strikes on you, you must guard that plate against the possibility of the pitcher's slipping a good pitch past you. You can guess all you want. Tell yourself that he is *sure* to waste a pitch. But don't count on it. Be ready to be surprised, or you may be left standing there with no more strikes due you.

In professional baseball, the pitchers do not hesitate to try to loosen a batter up, to move him back from the plate if he crowds it, or to keep him from digging in, especially after someone has just put a ball in the seats. The "bean ball" is supposed to be illegal, and if the pitcher throws at a batter two or three times in a row, he is very likely to be called on it by the umpire. Nevertheless, pitchers do throw at batters and probably always will. They may call the pitch a "brush-back" or a tight pitch. But make no mistake about it, if you do not move out of the way, it is going to hit you.

Still, you cannot let yourself be intimidated by this pitch. You should stand your ground until you see it is coming right at you, then bail right out without considering your dignity at all. Just hit the dirt and let him have his little victory (it counts for you anyway and if he does it again he is going to put himself in a hole). But when you dust yourself off, get right back in your regular position, even a little closer to the plate, and let him know by your stance that you are going to stay in there and hit. Don't try to make a personal vendetta out of it. It's part of the game. Pitchers will stop doing it only when you make it plain you are not going to be intimidated.

A pitcher wants to set the pace of the game and he may do so sometimes by making you wait in the batters' box while he decides what to throw. Or he may pretend to be shaking off his catcher's signs, just so he can cool you off or increase your nervousness. But don't let any such stuff throw you off stride. You have a right to ask for time. (You can't "call" time. Only the umpire can do that.) And you can step out of the box, use some dirt to dry your hands, and take a practice cut or two, so the pitcher has to wait for *you*. You can even ask the umpire to look at the ball to make sure it has not been doctored up with saliva or grease or dirt. But the best way is simply to remain cool and pay no heed to the delay unless it becomes unreasonable or you feel yourself tensing up.

The catcher may have tricks of his own to distract or upset you. Many catchers like to talk to batters to get their minds off the baseball or to break their concentration. Chat all you want to with the catcher. But once you have assumed your batting stance, pay him no mind. Fix your eye on the ball and let nothing distract you. While you may sometimes get advance notice of where the pitch is coming by noting, out of the corner of your eye, the position the catcher takes, bear in mind that catchers are given to misleading batters. A favorite trick is for the catcher to get out of his crouch and pound his fist into his glove up near your ear, pretending he is looking for a high pitch when he has actually called one low and outside. Take care not to be taken in by bush league tricks of this sort. You watch the baseball. That is what you have to hit. And center your mind on it with all your mental power.

The pitcher hopes of course to upset your timing by varying the speed of his pitches. If he can get you to step into the pitch too soon and swing at the ball too far in front of you, he has a good chance of getting you out. Your aggressive attitude therefore should not be allowed to turn into impatience. The batter who charges up to the plate and can't wait to get his bat on the ball is easy meat for the pitcher.

Of course much of your timing of pitches will come from experience. Without trying to figure it all out as the ball approaches, you will be able to judge the speed of the ball—provided you are giving it your full attention. There are always little things that help you know what is coming, and some of them may be things you do not consciously make note of at all—such as the way the pitcher brings his front foot down with an extra hard bang when he lets his fast ball go, or the manner in which he half loses balance for an instant. Your mind will take note of all these things if you give it a chance and will help you adjust to what is coming.

But as we pointed out earlier you should be ready if need be to correct yourself if you have been fooled on a pitch. Just because you have taken your stride, you are not required to go through with your swing. And if you discover that the ball is not where you thought it was going to be, you should *hold up*—hard!

You learn most about pitchers and catchers by playing against them in ballgames, for that is when they exhibit all their habits of strategy and play. Make a practice therefore of pursuing this study intently—all the time. If you are on the bench, you have a perfect spot from which to observe the pitcher's methods of holding the ball and delivering it. You can learn to recognize any tiny differences in his methods of throwing fast ball, curve, and change-up. Sometimes you can discover the giveaway move that tells when he has given up on the baserunner and is really throwing to the plate. You can learn to differentiate between a catcher's false moves and his real ones.

When you are in the on-deck circle, you can time the pitches, and observe the pitching pattern. You can also check on the pitcher's control. None of this time should be wasted if you want to learn how to hit. Of course, hitting practice is what you want most. But a thorough knowledge of the different ways pitchers and catchers are going to try to get you out will serve you well when your turn to bat comes up. So don't let your attention wander during a ball game, even if you are not going to do any more than pinch hit. You can be learning something every inning if you keep your eye on the ball and not on the girls in the stands.

Game Situations

Unless you are an unusually powerful guy with extra strong shoulders, forearms and wrists, who can drive baseballs out of the park or into the scoreboard with some regularity, there will be plenty of times during a ball game when you will be asked to follow strict instructions on when and how and where to hit the ball. And even if you are a home run hero, you may still come up against situations that demand bat control rather than sheer power. So nothing but good can come of learning how to use your bat so you have a good chance of placing the ball where it ought to be.

45

In school and amateur ball, the hit-and-run (really the run-and-hit) play is more talked about than used. It takes an experienced batter to hit behind the runner and amateurs seldom possess the experience. Of course if you bat left-handed, or switch, you will find it easier to get the ball behind the man who is going down from first to second. But a right-handed batter must learn to place the ball between first and second base too, because there is a useful and important play that requires hitting the ball on the ground to the right side of the infield.

When you have a man on second base with first base open and nobody out, you have a chance of getting a runner over where he can score on almost any sort of play—a long fly, an infield out, a bunt, a passed ball, a wild pitch. And there are many times in baseball when a single run is extremely important. When this situation arises in a game, your coach or manager is very likely to ask you to sacrifice a time at bat for the sake of getting that run over. He will not be asking you for a sacrifice bunt, which does not count as a time at bat, but for a ground ball to right that will give the runner a chance to make a third. (Since it is a tag play at third, the infielder, unless the runner is slow and the ball gets to the fielder with unusual speed, is going to make the play at first, to put you out, rather than chance missing the out altogether.)

Hitting the ball in the "opposite" direction requires a shorter grip on the bat and a shorter swing. You have to *wait* for the ball a fraction of a second longer, for if you hit the ball too far out front you are likely to foul up the whole play by delivering the ball to shortstop or the third baseman. But chiefly you hit it with an abbreviated swing. Instead of using the full arm swing and follow through, you bring the bat down sharply into the ball and allow your swing to fade away abruptly to the left. It is like the motion you would use to chop a notch in a tree—that is, you swing in a controlled, abbreviated way to make sure you meet the ball in the right spot. The shortness of your grip improves your aim.

The best ball for hitting to right is of course a curve ball, for that comes into the outer edge of the strike zone. An inside pitch is pretty difficult to put into the opposite field. But it can be done, if you open your stance enough to enable you to lay the heavy part of the bat on the ball. And if the pitcher knows of your intent, or suspects it, you can be sure he is going to try to keep the ball inside. Still, if it is in the strike zone, you should be able, by hitting it late with a shortened swing, to put it where you want it to go.

Baseball being a team game, maneuvers of this sort are always necessary at some point. They don't help your batting average. But if your batting average is more important to you than winning ball games, you are not going to stay very long on any club.

Even if you are a home run hitter whose mates

expect him to take his full cut every time in the hope of breaking the ball game open, you will still come up against situations that will make you wish you had practiced bat control. The confirmed pull hitters may find the defenses stacked against them. And the ability to drop a ball where there is nobody to field it can help persuade the opposition that this maneuver had best be abandoned.

Hitting the Knuckle Ball

Every hitter runs up against "unhittable" pitches, or at least pitches that are almost impossible for *him* to hit safely. These too are sometimes handled—if they cannot be avoided—by a shorter swing and shorter grip, to enable you to place the bat against the ball with more accuracy. Perhaps the one pitch most hitters most dislike is the knuckle ball, for it has so little momentum it seems to stand still in the air, then fade right away from the bat. Part of the knuckler's effectiveness is due to the fact that it creates an optical illusion of sorts. It pops out of the pitcher's hand as if it were going to speed right down to the plate, and because it does not spin and the seams are visible, it actually seems larger than a ball pitched in the regular way. As the eye adjusts to the fact that the ball is not approaching at normal speed, the ball seems to "hesitate" or "flutter." And near the plate it is likely to break in almost any direction.

48

To cope with this pitch, the batter needs a good long look at the ball. That means a more open stance, with the body turned a bit more toward the pitcher. A controlled swing then will enable you to hit this ball to the opposite field, which is the best place to try to hit a knuckler. If you try to pull the ball you are much more likely to be off in your timing, for trying to meet this pitch well in front of the plate means you do not have much time to gauge it and so will be more likely to hit it *after* you have completed your stride, with just a little arm strength, and off balance.

The Squeeze Play

The squeeze play is often used in the late innings of a game when the tying or winning run is on third and there are less than two out. Occasionally a manager or coach will go to the suicide squeeze, in which the runner commits himself as soon as the pitcher starts his pitch, and the batter is required to get his bat on the ball no matter where it is. The pitcher's way of dealing with this tactic is to throw the ball right at the batter, to force him to drop out of the box and enable the catcher to grab the ball and tag the runner. But the batter cannot surrender to this stunt. He should be ready to give ground if need be to stay in the box and get his bat on the ball, even if he only fouls it off, to protect the runner. Many pitchers do not observe the runner until too late to resort to this method, but they may succeed in getting the ball far out of the strike zone. All the same, it is the batter's job to get his bat on that ball, even if he has to throw his bat. There is no excuse for failing to do this, because the runner is a dead duck if the batter does not protect him.

On this play you must take extra care not to interfere with the catcher. If you do the *runner* will be called out, whether he has been tagged or not.

Of course most of the time on a suicide squeeze you get a ball you can bunt. Then your job is to get the ball on the ground in safe territory. Do not tap it too hard. The pitcher will be charging in to pick up the ball. If he does not get it in one stride, his chances of getting the runner out (unless the runner is a real slowboat) are about zero. But if you tap it where he can snatch it right up, he may put the runner out with a quick scooping toss to the catcher. Of course if you stiff-arm the bunt or try to bunt with a straight back, you may pop the ball into the pitcher's hands and into an easy double play.

The Sacrifice Fly

Bringing a man in from third base with a sacrifice fly does not require bat control so much as it does power to get the ball out where even a good throw will not beat the runner. Usually the batter

50

must wait for a high pitch to insure getting the ball in the air. But a man with a good uppercutting swing, in which the bat swoops down and then up, with the barrel of the bat somewhat lower than the handle, can get a low pitch into the air too. The danger here is that too much concern with where the ball will go may upset your concentration. You must be sure to keep your head from turning. Keep your eye right on the ball, sighting down the bat to see it, and let your natural swing take care of the rest.

The Safety Squeeze

The safety squeeze play is just a sacrifice bunt to bring in the man from third. In this play the runner goes only when the ball is safely on the ground. And of course it is the batter's job to put it on the ground, far enough from the plate so the catcher cannot recover it in time to tag the runner. The batter should square away on this play and not try to push or drag the bunt in order to turn it into a base hit. Just get out there in front of the box and get your bat in front of the ball, angling the bunt away from the pitcher so he cannot field it too quickly. Don't fret about the charging infielders. If you get the ball on the ground and do not tap it too sharply, they will have no chance of getting the runner. You will most likely be out, but do not concede this. Force them to make a fast play on you.

Batting Slumps

THE BEST BATTERS in the world hit periods now
and then when they cannot get a base hit for
money. A good part of the time the trouble is
psychological. That is, the batter has a streak
of seeing well hit balls go straight into fielders'
hands, and begins to fret about his stance and
his swing until he has himself out of the groove
completely. Or he begins to press, to jump at the
first pitch, to overswing, or to go for pitches out
of the strike zone. The more he does this, the
deeper the slump becomes, the more his confidence
becomes diluted and the less effective he is at the
plate.

Sometimes, of course, overconfidence can cause
a batter to grow careless about keeping his eye on
the ball, or about attacking the pitches with the
grim determination necessary. Or he may have
developed a fault that he has not even noticed.
Perhaps he is not cocking his wrists as he used to,
not recoiling enough, stepping a little away from
the pitch, not gripping his bat tightly enough,
lunging at the ball, turning his head too soon.

Once in a great while there may be some actual
physical difficulty. Batters in their late thirties
sometimes find that their eyes have actually un-
dergone a physical change—as human eyes do
near age forty—and that all they really need is a
pair of glasses.

It is also possible that you will go into a slump

when the pitchers discover a way of getting you out. There may be a certain pitch or a certain part of the strike zone that spells your weakness and the catchers and pitchers may be all taking advantage of the knowledge. This often happens when a good young hitter has been once around the circuit.

What you do about your slump then depends on what causes it. If you have been hitting consistently for a long time and have begun to go out on the pitches you used to cream, then it would not be wise to try to make any radical changes in your stance and swing. There will always be plenty of people to tell you to try this method or that. But if you have been getting good results over a long period of time, you had better stick to the method that has been working for you.

But make sure you have not developed some flaw, without realizing it. Have someone watch you at the plate for a while and tell you if you have fallen into any bad habits. Don't let them change your basic swing. But listen to what they have to say about possible weaknesses. If it makes sense to you, try to overcome the weakness.

But above all, *keep swinging*. Don't let good pitches go by because you are afraid you might look bad on them. Continue to attack the pitches you like—and don't be half-hearted about it. Don't be overeager or impatient. But *swing* at the good ones.

The way to cure a slump is to hit the ball and sometimes the best way to hit the ball may be to shorten your grip a little and shorten your swing. It would be better to do this than to whale away blindly at everything in the strike zone. Get a few fair balls out in the grass and your confidence will begin to bloom once more. There are hitters who think that to make up for the pitches they have been missing they must swing harder and harder. This is like playing for bigger and bigger stakes when you are having a bad run of luck. You are not going to "get even" by getting a lucky home run. You are going to come back by getting your bat on the ball and hitting it safely.

Now and then it turns out that a batting slump has its origin in something that has nothing to do with baseball—a domestic difficulty, an emotional upset of some sort, worry over finances, over family or, in the case of youngsters, over school. There are hundreds of things in a batter's life that may chip away at his concentration. If you remember that really *fierce* concentration is needed at the plate you will realize that you cannot afford to use time between pitches to think about what you might have said or ought to say to this guy or that, or to stew about some quarrel that has not been settled. All outside matters must be brutally shoved out of your mind while you center on getting your bat on the ball.

Some hitters who are having tough luck at the plate try to blame all their troubles on someone else. Someone has given them wrong advice. Someone has broken their pet bat. Someone kept them awake last night. Someone scolded them too harshly or interfered with their fun or humiliated them before their teammates. When a batter starts to figure along these lines he is just feeling sorry for himself and soon will be actually enjoying his misery, until his slump becomes deeper and deeper. What he needs then is to grab himself by the scruff of the neck and shake some sense back into his skull. Or perhaps he needs the coach or manager to deliver a sudden sharp boot in the seat of the pants—a figurative one, of course.

Whatever you do to overcome your failures at the plate, do not let yourself begin to "take" good pitches because they are less than perfect. If a pitcher can get you out by just throwing the ball through the strike zone, why should he *ever* throw a pitch you want to see? It is up to you to protect that plate and not make life too easy for the pitcher. This does not mean you should not take a strike now and then to size the pitcher up, or to wait for a better one. But don't put yourself in a hole through fear of missing the ball.

A great many good hitters in the world have turned failure into success just through determination. Sometimes a batter has had to go back to the minors and learn his job all over again. Pitchers after all are just as determined to get you out as you are to hit the ball safely and they are not going to let you get away with some batting weakness in the big time. You are going to have to work and sweat and suffer to overcome that weakness. You may have to undergo the humiliation of dropping right back down the ladder and climbing the last few rungs all over again. Even Mickey Mantle had to go back to the minor leagues—where he got one hit in his first *twenty-three* times at bat!—in order to become better acquainted with his strike zone. The good athletes come back because they are determined to make good and are not too pigheaded to listen to advice.

Practice and Practice

ORDINARY "BATTING PRACTICE" that a fellow takes before a game will not provide practice enough to develop a really good hitter. To hit well, you have to practice almost continuously, at least when you are young—practice in all your off time, practice the year around. If you are not in a place where you can actually swing a bat against thrown balls, you can at least practice swinging—something. Practice swinging a rolled-up newspaper. Practice with an umbrella or a broomstick. Study yourself in the mirror as you swing. Make sure you are doing all the things you want to do and that you follow through smoothly and completely on your swing.

As for actually batting a pitched baseball, you are going to have to find someone willing to throw you the ball hour after hour—after games, before games, in between games, before the season starts and after it is over. The best batters in the game have beaten out thousands and thousands of baseballs in practice.

First practice on balls that are easy to hit and hit a lot of them. Then, after you have found your best stance and swing, and developed your confidence, work on the balls that you find hard to hit and hit a lot of *those*. But remember it is by hitting, and not by missing, that you learn the job. Don't keep hitting against a guy who is trying to get you out. Batting practice is for *hitting*.

But there are other aspects of the job that require strengthening of muscles and special exercises and conditioning. Your general physical condition can affect your hitting, just as your general physical strength will determine how much power you can put into your batting swing. It is worth noting that guys who have done a lot of work with their arms and hands—or who have gone in for an extraordinary amount of physical exercise—are often the best hitters. Swinging a hammer or an axe, pulling an oar, working with a hoe and all similar work is good batting practice in a way for it builds up muscles in shoulders, forearms, and wrists that you will use when you swing a baseball bat.

Swinging a bat against resistance is a good way of adding strength and power. The ideal way of course is to use the bat to hit baseballs. But there are times when you just cannot get out and hit. Then you can get good results by hitting a sandbag with a bat, or pounding on a spare tire. You can hang some such thing in your cellar or your garage, or somewhere else where there is not room enough for baseball. Put a mark on it for a target and then swing hard at it with a baseball bat. Exercise of this sort will also toughen your hands, so you can get a good strong grip on the bat handle.

Conditioning

As for your general condition, the best conditioning exercise in the world is *running*—not jogging, running. You can do that in city or country. Good strong legs are an asset to you at the plate, on the baselines, and in the field. Also running will expand your lungs, strengthen your heart, improve your circulation, add to your endurance. Try to do some running every day. Don't just trot around in a circle once or twice. Run hard. Run uphill and downhill. Run until you feel the effort. Run until the sweat pours and the breath comes hard. Only in that way will you really condition your body. Of course, meanwhile you will lay off smoking and overeating and anything else that will shorten your breath, add excess flab to your frame, or cut your endurance. A batter who cannot run is not much of a batter because if you cannot reach first base in good time you are going to lose a lot of base hits.

Good hands and a good grip are also vital to a batter. Swinging a bat will strengthen and toughen your hands. But a batting glove may help your grip too, by eliminating soreness and blisters. And simple squeezing of a rubber ball day after day will add a lot of oomph to your grip.

Determination

More than physical fitness a batter needs mental determination. Learning to do this hardest of all athletic jobs (and one of the most satisfying after you have learned it) requires the facing down of a whole lot of discouragement. Many a "natural" hitter who has cost the home team a few boxes of baseballs in school competition and in amateur or semi-pro soon loses his heart when professional pitchers bring him the news that he cannot hit a curve. And too many of these guys, after madly flailing the air to try to make the baseball go the way it used to, throw up their hands in despair and quit the game altogether. Every major league club has had youngsters on its roster who looked like world beaters until the day when the pitchers started throwing curves. A big league curve is no sweeping, flat job but a sharp off-the-table change in direction that moves down and away at the same time. Just getting the bat out on a level with the pitch does not mean you are going to hit it and a whole lot of practice is needed to adjust to the ball's move and get the bat on it.

A really determined young man, when he runs up against an obstacle like this, will start trying to figure out ways of overcoming it. It may take weeks, months, even years to do it. A number of good hitters who posted fat averages in the minors tumbled into the low .200's in the majors and had to go back and spend a season or two more getting ready to hit big league pitching. Getting to the top that way, then falling off, is an experience that requires an extra amount of guts and application to live through. As a matter of fact, staying on top, when pitchers are trying their best to find ways of putting you out, requires constant application to the job and everlasting practice. There is no such thing these days as the home town hero who does his training only in the local tavern and starts hitting when the game begins. Even the best of batters learn to live year round with that baseball bat as a marine learns to live with his rifle. They hit whenever and wherever there is opportunity and they never stop studying the pitchers and catchers, to familiarize themselves with the patterns that will be used against them.

Running the Bases

A PROFESSIONAL BASEBALL player starts to run the bases while he is still in the on-deck circle. That is, he goes over the signs in his mind to make sure he has them straight. (If he is doubtful he checks with the coach *before* he bats.) He notes the positions of the fielders and reminds himself too of where the strong arms are and which man, if any, has the weak arm. He also considers what may happen if the man ahead of him gets on base. What is the hit-and-run sign he has with this man? What may he be asked to do? After that he pays close attention to the pitcher, to see what sort of ball he is throwing and what his control is like.

The man becomes a baserunner as soon as he hits a fair ball, or gets a free ride to first through being walked or being hit by a pitch. If he hits the ball, he does not wait to see who fields it or where it goes. He can trust the umpire to tell him if the ball is fair (unless of course it is an obvious foul). But the runner's first rule is *hustle*. Fans and managers both like to see a ballplayer *run* to first, no matter how slim the chance is that he will make it. Running to first on a base on balls gives a good impression too. (And sometimes it even pays off in an extra base, if ball four has got by the catcher.)

Running to First

Running to first, you must stay *off* the baseline. Your course is in foul ground, outside the line. If you run directly on the line, particularly if the ball is behind you, you are likely to be called for interference.

Run across first base without breaking stride.

If the play at first is likely to be close, run straight for the bag, and stick to your full stride all the way. Do not make the mistake of attempting a flying leap for the bag. You will find that breaking your stride to make such a jump actually slows you down. Put on all the speed you've got and run right across the bag without breaking stride at all.

If the ball is hit to the outfield make note while

you are running of where it is going. Start your turn for second *before* you reach first base. That is, swing out to your right and tag the *inside* corner of the bag, then start straight up the baseline toward second base. If the fielder bobbles the ball, or has not retrieved it, you just keep on going, *straight* for the bag if second is going to be your base. But if the ball has gone past the fielders, you have to start your turn for third before you get to second. Do not wait for the coach to signal you on. You have to be *on your way* to third before you

Tagging the inside corner.

reach second or you may not beat the throw. So again you swing out before reaching the bag, tag the inside corner and head straight for third.

When you are running down from first to second, do not forget to look to see what is happening with the ball. You do not have to worry about obstacles when you are running on a baseball diamond, so you can take your eyes off the ground long enough to check the position of the baseball. Will there be a throw to second? Will you have to slide? These are questions you must decide for

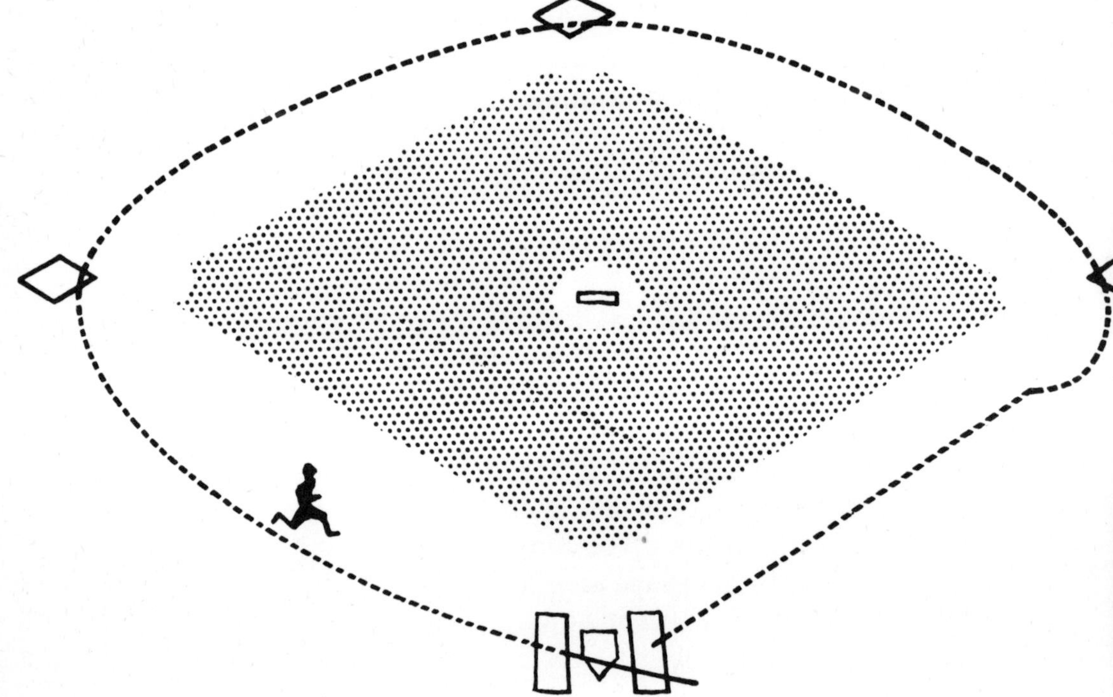

Running all out on all the bases.

yourself as you watch the way the ball is fielded. You may even have to scramble back to first base if the ball has been handled with special swiftness. But never concede that until you have to. Be *aggressive* on the bases. Don't be foolhardy or take silly chances. But look for that extra base whenever there is the slightest chance you may get it. A throw may be wild. An outfielder may flub an easy ground ball. An infielder may have wandered out of position and left a base unguarded. If any of those things happen, you want to be ready to take advantage of them.

It is this alertness, combined with aggressiveness, that makes a valuable baserunner. Sheer speed is not enough on the bases. Some of the best base runners have not been the fastest men in the game at all. But they have been men who have used their eyes and their brains, who always knew just what the score was, just how many were out, just where the ball was.

If you have stopped at first and are looking for a way to get to second, you have to check the situation carefully. Above all, you should know where the rightfielder is playing. He will be out of your sight as you stand on the baseline, so you should check to see where he is. Then you will *know*, if the ball is hit in his direction, whether it is going beyond him, to his glove side, to his barehand side, or in front of him. (If it is going to his glove side, it will take him longer to get off a throw.) If he is playing far from the foul line, then a ball hit down the line will probably send you to third. If he is back against the wall, a short fly is going to fall safe, and you can take off.

Of course you will also know the score and the outs. You will know if you represent the tying or lead run or if your club is several runs behind and you must play it safe in hopes of building a rally.

Stealing Second

If you plan to steal second, you have to know the pitcher's moves. Go over in your mind what you know about him—and decide what chances you can take. The standard lead off base is the length of your body plus a step. That is, you go just as far as you can and still get back with a dive, in case the pitcher's move catches you there. Now take a look at your coach and see if he is giving you a sign. Do not make the bush league mistake of looking away as soon as he gives the sign. Big league signs are simple but they are surrounded by fake signs and you must take care not to reveal when the *real* sign has been given.

You do not move away from the base until the pitcher is on the mound and ready to pitch. (He cannot take his position on the mound without the ball.) Now if you are to steal second base, you have got to run some risk. You cannot wait until the ball is on the way to the plate. Then you will not have time enough. You have got to start *before* the pitcher goes to the plate. You can understand now the advantage of knowing the little telltale move or sign that indicates the pitcher has given up on you and is going to throw to the batter.

66

Intensive study of the pitcher's moves will pay off in a jump of two or three strides.

When the pitcher is left-handed, you may have to take a good deal less than your normal lead. On a right-hander, if you have quick reflexes you may be able to stretch the lead an extra step. But in any case, never take your eyes off the pitcher after you have taken your lead. Move away from the base with care, ready to jump or dive back, and when you have got your lead stand with legs apart and knees flexed, watching every move the pitcher makes. There are a few runners who stroll away from the base and keep moving until the pitcher stops them. But it is safest to edge away carefully.

When the pitch is released, you should always take a few quick steps up the line, increasing your

The perfect lead-off will allow you to dive back to the base.

lead. But do not be reckless about this. Stay near enough (unless you are actually taking off for second) to get back if the catcher throws to the bag. When the ball is hit, you want to have as good a start as you can get away with. It may mean that extra base, even a score. But if the ball is not hit, move back toward the bag. Do not be caught away up the line, with no place to go.

Your stance, as you prepare to steal, should be alert and poised, on the balls of your feet, with your knees bent. You should be ready to jump off the mark in an instant. Whether you start with a cross-over step or with a step by the foot nearest second does not matter. Do whatever comes most natural to you. But remember, you have to take a chance on a steal. You cannot wait until the ball is on its way. If you do not know the motion that gives away the pitcher's intent, then you will just have to guess, and hope you guess right. If you are wrong, of course you will probably be picked off first. But that is the price you pay for running risks. And the gain of an extra base—eliminating a double-play possibility and putting you ninety feet closer to home plate—is often worth considerable risk. But if you are unable to get a good jump on the pitcher, stay put. A good jump is what makes a base-stealing champion. Speed alone won't help you if you fail to get that one-second start that the jump provides. When the coach gives you the steal sign, he means for you to get a jump on the pitcher.

There are times when you break for second without getting a jump. But these are not rated as steals. When the count is three and two on the batter and two men are out, you start for second as soon as the ball is on its way. No need to try for the jump in these circumstances because unless the batter hits a foul he is either going to walk or make the third out, and you will either be automatically safe at second or the inning will be over.

The Hit-and-Run Play

Then there is the hit-and-run play, or run-and-hit play. On this, you break for second only when the pitch is on the way. It is up to the batter to protect you by hitting the ball. And it is up to *you* to make sure the ball is on the ground. You should never, never, *never* get doubled up on a fly ball on the hit-and-run play. No matter how fast you are moving, you can afford a quick glance at the plate to see if the ball has been hit on the ground. If it has been popped up, then you must scramble back to first. It is the same way on a sacrifice. You should never be doubled up because a bunt has turned into a pop fly and been caught. You can make sure the ball is on the ground before you go all the way. If it is not—*back* you go—*fast!* Make a habit on these plays of looking back at the plate as you take off. A quick glance is enough to tell you what has happened to the ball. If the batter hits a line drive, you must hold up a split second to make sure it is going through.

You can also, on rare occasions, advance to second base after a long fly has been caught. But it usually requires a long, long fly and a mediocre arm on the fielder, because you are running *toward* the ball. Ordinarily on a fly ball you do not tag up but go halfway down the line toward second, ready to cut loose if the fielder drops or misplays the ball.

Sliding

When you get to second, you cannot run straight across it as you can at first. If the play is even reasonably close, you want to keep yourself from overrunning the bag, so you slide. The best slide under these circumstances is what ballplayers call the pull-up slide. To perform this slide, you go straight at the bag, facing it directly, and not turning your body. You bend one leg and coast in on the shin and foot of the bent leg. The other foot is straight out in front of you, and you use it to tag the bag. The underneath leg, on which you slide, must be bent at right angles to the other leg with the underneath foot under the other thigh. If you do not roll your body to one side or the other (and you should never do that) you will be in a position, after you reach the bag, to pull yourself quickly erect and go on to third if the ball has got away.

Sometimes you will see a runner using this slide put one hand down into the dirt to steady himself. This is a dangerous stunt. You can easily

70

break a finger or jam a thumb this way and put yourself out of the lineup. You must train yourself to go in straight up, as if you were just suddenly sitting down. Throw your hands in the air over your head to make sure you do not put them in the ground. For many years baserunners have made a habit of picking up two handfuls of dirt, which they throw away as they slide, thus reminding themselves to get those hands over the head.

Sliding does not speed up your arrival at a base but it does make it more difficult to put a tag on you and it will sometimes enable you to unbalance the fielder long enough to make it impossible for

The pull-up slide.

71

him to get a throw off in time to nail the hitter at first. You use a very different slide on these occasions. In one instance, you want to offer as little of your body as possible to the fielder to tag. In the other, you want to come right into the fielder, so he has got to jump out of your way.

The slide you use to avoid a tag is the hook slide, for you just hook the base with your toe, thus offering only your toe and lower leg to be tagged. To perform this slide successfully you have to slide away from the fielder, so of course you must keep your eye on him as you approach the bag and you must have practice in sliding either to right or left of the bag.

In the hook slide you slide on your hip, actually

The hook slide.

aiming your slide away from the bag and letting your toe catch the bag as you go by it. You aim one foot to the side of the base away from the fielder and slide on the hip on that side (with your hands up!). So instead of bending the underneath leg at right angles as in the pull-up slide, you stick it out straight, to go past the base. The upper leg is bent so the foot just drags along to catch the base as you go by.

When you are trying to break up a double play there is of course a force out at second and so there is no need to avoid a tag. You just go straight on the side of the bag where the fielder is taking his position. Of course if he gets the ball well ahead of you and gets far off the bag, you cannot chase him into the infield. But as long as he is on the bag or close to it or on the baseline,

Breaking up the double play.

you have a perfect right to cross that territory. It belongs to you as a baserunner. The rules prevent you from deliberately interfering with a fielder. But if the fielder takes a position on *your* territory, you are not required to surrender it to him. So you slide right in straight at his feet so he must jump, or hop aside, or get out of your path somehow. Often this sudden move on his part will delay his throw, or get it off target, or even prevent it altogether, so the men at first will be safe. Now and then he may try to hold his ground and there will be a collision, tumbling him on top of you. No experienced fielder is going to get angry about this (unless you have actually run off the baseline to "get" him). He will try the same thing himself when *he* is running bases. And the baserunner who will not at least make an effort to break up a double-play throw will not earn any good marks from his manager.

Sliding is an important part of baseball and it deserves a good deal of practice. There was a time when all ballplayers wore sliding pads under their uniforms but no one bothers with them any more. Instead, they wear underwear that reaches most of the way to the knee and count on that and the heavy uniform pants to cut down on the "strawberries" that a slide will sometimes raise. It is just as well, however, not to practice your sliding on the baselines, because you can scrape your hide unnecessarily in that way, especially if you do not know how to place your legs properly.

Probably the easiest place to practice sliding, and the most fun, is in wet grass. You'll get your clothes a little damp that way but you will find the actual sliding easy and you can practice your controlled fall without danger of taking a few inches of hide off your hip or thigh. There are not too many sliding pits available for practice but grass is available nearly everywhere. You do not even need to use a base at the beginning because the important thing is to learn to let yourself go into the slide without hitch or hesitation.

Changing your mind about sliding or deciding to slide too late can both be dangerous. If you hesitate too long or try to "catch" yourself, you may get your weight too close to the base and as a result go into a bad tumble instead of a slide. You can wrench a knee or twist an ankle this way. So take care that when you decide to slide you go through with it quickly. Do not wait until you are on top of the base. And do not try to stop a slide once you have committed yourself to it.

It is good too to get into the habit of turning your feet slightly upward when you slide. Just pretend you are trying to keep the soles of your shoes from getting dirty and you will always avoid catching a spike in the ground as you slide. A bad injury can result if a spike catches, for the whole weight of your body as it flies forward will be pressing against your twisted ankle. It is a very simple matter to keep your soles turned away from the ground as you slide along. Make a constant habit of it.

Base to Base

ONCE YOU HAVE reached second base safely, you have a new set of problems. You take a different sort of lead off second. And there are two fielders close by, either one of whom can put a tag on you.

First of all you must be sure where the ball is. Often in the confusion of slide and recovery, or after a close play and a collision, you will lose track of the ball completely. You should look for the ball first of all. Do not leave the base until you *know* where the baseball is. Look to the outfield. Perhaps it got away from the fielder and you can take off at once for third. Look to see if the shortstop or second basemen has it. Look at the pitcher. If he is staying off the mound, then you stay *on* the base, unless you can see the ball in his hand.

With the ball back in the pitcher's hand, you can begin to take your lead off the base. You will be able to see the second basemen and take care that you do not get farther away from the base than he is. The shortstop will be behind you and the coach at third will be yelling to you to tell where he is. But do not count on the coach entirely. First take a quick look yourself and be sure you have him placed.

There is not much percentage, especially if you are not a speedster, in taking too long a lead off second base. Of course with the pitch you will move a few steps toward third. But do not move blindly. Do not turn and trot away from the base. Slide along, the way a boxer does, moving the right foot first and bringing the left up, keeping your eye on the ball meanwhile. If you get too far away and lose track of the ball, the catcher can snap a throw down to second and trap you.

On a fly ball to deep outfield, a long lead will not give you any advantage. You can go halfway anyway as the ball goes to the outfield and you can watch to see what happens. If it looks as if it is sure to be caught, you can hustle back to tag up and then try for third if you think you can make it. (And if the base is open!) This is a time when you must depend on your own judgment. If you wait for the coach to tell you when to try, you are very likely to start too late.

If the ball is hit ahead of you, on the ground, hold back until you are *sure* it is through. Do not run into an out. But do not tell yourself you can never advance on a ground ball hit in front of you. Watch the ball! If it gets by a fielder, or even if it pulls the third basemen or shortstop far out of position, you may be able to make it to third. Here again you must use your own judgment. Stay alert and aggressive. You should never doze off on the baselines. You are as much in the game as the hitter is and you must keep your eye on the ball just as earnestly as he does.

If a ground ball goes to the right side of the diamond—to first or second baseman that is—you may have a good chance to make third, unless the ball is an easy roller or a line drive into the fielder's hands. You *must* make sure about this. Do not just dig for third on a ball hit to right. Be sure first that it is past the infielder, that it has not been taken on the fly, or that it is a hard enough chance to keep him busy making the out at first. You can usually judge this in a flash. But don't take it for granted.

A fly ball may be long enough to bounce off the fence. When you are on second base you should *not* take right off on a fly that looks as if it will hit the fence. Wait for a second on that kind of blow and see what comes of it. Maybe it will get away from everyone and you can go all the way home. Maybe it will rocket back toward the infield and you will not be able to advance.

On second base, you have got to do a lot of thinking. You must be well aware of the score and the number of outs. If the ball that is hit is going to make out number two, there is not much sense in taking a long chance on advancing, because it will still take a safe hit to score you even from third base. And a safe hit will probably score you from second.

Don't be in a rush to start for third on a bunt either. You are not forced to advance if first base is open, and you should use your head about advancing. If a ball is bunted and fielded quickly, you could be caught at third. The fielders are going to be awake to the idea of picking you off if they can, so you must be awake too.

A long lead off second base often means that the pitcher and catcher will keep you "leaning" toward second by faking pick-offs. And if you are leaning toward second base when the ball is hit, you are not going to get as good a start as you should.

78

Do not take long chances on an advance from second when you do not represent a crucial run— the tying or winning run. If your side is several runs behind and you are likely to make the third out if you try to advance, it is just not worth it. Better stay where you are and let your side keep on hitting.

When you do advance to third on a hit baseball, keep alive to the possibility of going further. If a throw is coming in to second base there is always a chance it will get by the fielder. On a long blow, swing out as you approach third and glance back for the ball. If it has been fielded, you can apply the brakes and hold third. If it gets by the fielder, you may be able to keep right on going for home.

It is to your advantage too, when the ball has been fielded across the diamond, or in the far outfield, to draw a throw by rounding the base and going part way down the baseline. Do not go so far that you can't get back in a quick dive or jump. But do not go back until they try for you, or until the ball is brought too close to the bag for you to beat a throw back. And always be *sure* where the ball is before you get off the bag. Do what the coach tells you. But do not depend on him to tell you everything. *You* look for the ball and be sure where it is.

On Third

Assume now that you are on third base, with just ninety feet more to travel before you stop being a baserunner and become a run for your side. First of all, take your lead off third in foul territory. Do not run on the baseline. If you are hit by a batted ball in fair territory you will be out. But there is no play if you are hit by a foul ball. Take your lead depending on the distance from the bag that the third baseman plays. Do not get farther away than he is from third. Keep him in the corner of your eye as you watch the pitcher. Ordinarily as the pitcher prepares to throw the third basemen will move away from the bag. Then you can move toward home plate as the pitcher starts his motion. If the bases are full, the pitcher will often take a full wind-up, and while he winds up you can move slowly, just walking or shuffling, toward home plate. When he releases the ball, you break for home. You will stop short before you get past the point from which you will be able to get back safely. But faking a dash for home will distract both pitcher and catcher and give the batter an edge.

If the ball is hit to an infielder, unless the fielders are drawn in to cut off the run, you can sometimes make it home. In this again you have to use your own judgment, for by the time the coach could give you the word, it would be too late to start. If you get a good jump with the pitch and the ball is hit fairly deep you have a good chance of getting home. But if there are less than two out and you do not represent either the winning or the tying run, there is no point in taking long chances.

Sometimes, however, if you make a good hard fake for home on a ball hit to the infield, you can bluff the fielder into throwing to the plate. You put your head down and dig for home as the ball gets to the fielder, but you do so with the determination to stop short (you can get a quick stop by suddenly lowering your tail) and plunge back to the bag. If you are agile and can put on a good act, you may succeed in getting the fielder to try for you, while the batter gets safely to first, thus saving an out and providing still another chance for the blow that will bring you in.

With one out, you will probably be expected to try to score on any ground ball. To do this, you need a moving start so that by the time the pitch has reached the plate, you will be well on your way—except that you will still not go so far or run so hard as to be unable to scramble back if the ball gets by the batter. Even with a drawn-in infield, a slow bunt or a high-hopping ground ball may provide a chance to score, so you should get your start anyway, keep your eye on the ball and try for home *hard* if you have a chance. If by any chance a throw home does beat you, you should not count yourself out. Stop, start back, and keep yourself alive just as long as you can by faking and dodging. You may at least be able to allow the other runner to advance. When you are returning to third base, you run in *fair* ground, because in that way you create problems for the catcher. He has to take care not to hit you with his throw. And the third baseman may have a harder time getting a clear view of the coming ball.

There is sometimes an advantage in not *hurrying* home. When the ball is hit well enough, you may want to try to draw a throw so as to keep the batter from being cut down. This is a matter of judgment and of knowledge of your own speed. Naturally you do not want to chance being thrown out.

An attempt to score after a sacrifice fly is also a matter of judgment. You are a better judge than the coach of just how deep a fly must be to give you a chance to score. (But you should have some knowledge too of the throwing ability of the fielder who makes the catch.) Here again you cannot wait for the coach to give you the word about starting. You should watch the ball yourself so you will know when to start. You cannot leave the base until the ball has reached the fielder's glove. But you can start before that. You can steal an extra half second by taking your first step with the foot that is off the base, leaving one foot on as you start and starting just before the ball hits the glove. In this way, the other foot will not leave the base until the ball has been caught. But you will still have a flying start. If you wait until the coach gives you the word to "Go!" you will lose that fraction of a second and that may be the difference between safe and out.

Sometimes of course you come into third without being sure if you will have a chance to score. A throw is coming. The ball is behind you and if the throw is off target you will have a chance to keep going. So as you go into the base you use your pull-up slide, ready to come right to your feet and try for home if the ball gets by the baseman or the throw is wild. (But be sure you see the ball!) The

pull-up slide also creates problems for the fielders.
Your body, coming straight into the base, will ob-
struct the throw and the baseman's view of the
ball. Sometimes a throw, straight at the base, will
hit the runner in these circumstances and provide
a chance to keep going. A thrown ball is not going
to hurt you especially unless it hits you on the
head. Many base runners wear their helmets as
they run the bases so that if they do get in the way
of a throw, they are not going to be hurt by it.

The Double Steal

If the manager decides, while you are the runner at third, to pull a double steal, you have to
play your part carefully. On a double steal you
do not start for home until the catcher throws to
get the runner who is going down to second. Now
you are in the same position as if you were stealing second base—with the exception that you have
to guess with the catcher rather then the pitcher.
That is, you have to start *before* he actually lets
the ball go, or you will not have time to score. So
you break for the plate as soon as the catcher
cocks his arm for the throw to second. Maybe it is
a bluff. Then you will lose your gamble. Maybe he
will throw straight to the pitcher, or to an infielder cutting in to take the throw short of the
base. Again you lose your gamble.

But even then you do not call yourself out. The
other runner by this time will be on second and if

you can keep from being put out immediately, he may be able to get to third, and your team will not be much worse off. At least it will still have a man ninety feet away from a score.

Your value to your team increases greatly when you are at third base with nobody out. There are many ways in which you can be brought home— a safe blow, a ground ball to a deep infielder, a bunt, a sacrifice fly, a double steal, a wild pitch, a passed ball, a bad throw on a steal of second, etc. So you do not take any long chances. You do not want to become out number one any more than you want to become out number three. So you stay alert, keep your eye on the ball and try for home only when you feel sure you have a good chance. If the ball is hit in the air, you wait to see if it is going to be caught. If it is hit on the ground, of course you make your start for home, but you do not turn on the full juice until you see the ball has gone through or has gone deep enuogh to let you get in.

If there is a man on first and he tries to steal, even with no double steal signal, you can help him with a good fake of a double steal. A convincing dig for home may make the catcher hold up his throw for a second and this may give the other runner the edge he needs.

Stealing Home

Stealing home is a very rare event indeed. Many a good runner will go through a long career and never once steal home. But if you are blessed with the ability to get a fast start and can accelerate immediately, this is a stunt that can sometimes win a game. It usually works only when the pitcher gets careless about checking your lead. Keep your eye on the pitcher, as you edge away or walk away from third. If he fails to look over at you, keep taking a little more (keep one eye on the third baseman too, so as not to let him move too close to the bag). Then when the pitcher has committed himself to the pitch, you break hard for home and go in fast with a slide. If the catcher gets the ball while straddling the plate, the pull-up slide, with the lead foot aimed right between the catcher's feet, will work best. If he jumps out in front or stands behind the plate, you use your fall-away slide to hook the plate with your toe and give him as little body as possible to put the tag on.

You really cannot change your mind on a steal of home, so it is something to try only when all circumstances are favorable and when you know you can get off the mark with a bang and have a really good lead and topnotch speed.

Naturally a score can come when the catcher fails to hang on to a pitch. You have to watch that ball as devotedly as the batter does and decide in a flash if the ball has rolled far enough away to give you a chance to make your score. The pitcher will be covering the plate on this play, with his back to you as he waits the throw, and so the fall-away slide will be the best one to get you out of reach of a tag.

Don't forget that you can also score after a caught *foul* fly. Sometimes an outfielder will have his back to the plate as he goes after such a fly and he will be in a bad position for throwing when he makes the catch. (Outfielders often will not try for difficult foul flies with a man on third because the man will probably score.)

Just because an outfield fly does not look long enough to score on is no reason why you should just stand at third base and watch the ball game. You should be ready to move if anything goes wrong. And sometimes you can help things to go wrong for the other side. Occasionally outfielders do drop easy flies and you do not want to be caught asleep when this happens. Sometimes a careless outfielder will just lob a throw into the diamond. This also may enable you to score and you should be ready for it. Or when the outfielder has the ball you may be able to fake your way home by pretending to start hard for home, while watching the outfielder. He may fire the ball home, in which case you will get back to the base. Or he may make the mistake of bluffing a throw, when you have taken a good start. Then, unless you are a real slowboat on the bases, you have a good chance of getting home, for if he makes a bluff throw it will take him an extra second to wind back and make a real throw. That second will be just what you need to score provided you keep on going *fast*. You have to be moving at *controlled* speed (ready to stop and scramble back if he really lets the ball go) when he makes the fake, and really turn on full speed when you see it is a bluff.

Oftentimes you will be trying to score from bases other than third. That is, on a long blow you may head home from second or even first. Or a misplay in the outfield may provide you a chance to go all the way. So you should *watch the ball* as you speed along the baselines. The time to decide to try for home is when you are leaving second or when you are rounding second. You should start your turn for home *before* you get to third base, swinging out wide as you near the base, then toeing the inside corner of the base (crossing the middle of the base can cause you to trip or stumble—and it makes the route a bit longer).

Again you do not wait for the coach to tell you to try to score. But you do obey him. As you approach third, the coach will probably be part way down the line toward home where you can pick him out easily as you make your turn and head *straight* for the plate. He will flag you if he wants you to stop and scramble back.

You do not have to worry about overrunning home plate. Just be sure you hit it with foot or hand. Keep coming at top speed. You will use the slide, as suggested, depending on where the catcher is and how best to avoid his tag. But if the play at home is a force play (as from a base-full situation) you come in full speed and you *do not slide*. Even if the throw has you beaten you tear full tilt across the plate. Your headlong approach and your body passing in front of the catcher may keep him from completing a double play. There should never be any surrender on a play at the plate.

Good Baserunning

A good baserunner has to use his head at all times, as well as his speed. No baserunner should ever rip along oblivious of where the ball is, or what the score is. There are all kinds of opportunities to help your side as you run the bases and all kinds of chances to do your team some damage. You should never allow yourself to take for granted that a ball hit in the air will not be caught. No baserunner should ever be guilty of being doubled up on a line drive to the outfield, or on a popped-up bunt. You should always watch the ball, even as you move, and be sure it is on the ground before you shift into high speed. Few things can take the heart out of a team the way a line-drive double play can, when there are potential runs on the bases.

But there are also opportunities sometimes to take an extra base without much danger. Occasionally, even on a base on balls, somebody may forget the ball is alive, and will fail to move over to cover second base. Now and then when the catcher snaps the ball back to the pitcher, the shortstop may have forgotten to back him up and the ball will go through far enough to allow you to reach the next base. On throws from the outfield, the pitcher may neglect to back up the third baseman and an overthrow may keep right on going. When these things happen, even though they happen once in a thousand times, you should be ready to take advantage of them. The coaches on the baselines will remind you of the outs and the score and tell you what to watch out for. The manager or the coach may give the signal to steal. But they cannot do your thinking for you or tell you soon enough when you have a chance to advance.

There is even a delayed steal that may take advantage of a catcher's habit of lobbing the ball back to the pitcher. This does not often happen in the big leagues. But if ever you come up against a catcher who is lazy about getting the ball to the pitcher, and does not check your lead after a pitch, you may get away with grabbing second base if you take off just as the catcher lets the ball go. Sometimes the pitcher will not even know what is happening in this sort of play and may commit an error. Then your side will earn the reward of wide awake and aggressive baserunning.

Aggressive baserunning however does not mean just breaking loose with all the speed you've got whenever you get a jump. Sometimes you may have missed something—as when an outfield throw gets by the relay man and is picked up by the man who *backs up* the relay man. Or, once in a dozen years (and this has happened even in the big leagues) there may be a man ahead of you who is *not* running to the next base. Occasionally you may head for third and find that the man on third did not assess the chances in the same way, or was held up by the coach, and you will be one too many runners for that base to hold.

Of course you can avoid this disaster if you take care as you round second to pick up the third base coach (he will be about halfway down the baseline on this play) and see if he is holding up the man ahead of you or if he is signaling him to come ahead. But if you should get to a base and find a teammate there ahead of you, remember that the base belongs to him and you can be put out by being tagged with the ball even if you have your foot on the base. It is up to you to try to save the day by scrambling right back where you came from, and by trying to dodge and retreat and twist away from a tag as long as possible. Sometimes a potential disaster like this has been turned into a run when a throw is dropped or the man trying to get you out forgets the other runner, who dashes in to score.

In recent years in the major leagues it has even happened that a man has been out on the baselines after hitting a fair ball over the fence. How? By absentmindedly running past a teammate who was on base ahead of him. So even if you are prancing along rejoicing in a grand-slammer, don't go to sleep. The guy ahead of you may not have your speed. He may have stumbled. He may be just jogging while you are sprinting. He has got to score first or your run will not even count.

Sometimes, as in the late innings of a game when your club needs many runs, there is hardly any advantage in risking an out just to get an extra base. Only if you are the winning or the tying run will it be worth a risk to get closer to scoring position. When there is a lead to make up, then it is more important that your side stays at bat than that you move up a base. That is why managers insist that you *know* what the score is and how many are out at all times, even when you are on the bench.

If you are a good runner, you may be called on almost any time to go out on the baselines and you should go out there ready to use your brain as well as your speed.

The Winning Attitude

IN TALKING OF both batting and baserunning you will note we keep using the word aggressive. Being aggressive does not mean being a wise guy or throwing your weight around every time you appear in the diamond. It means going into a contest with the determination to win it, and going into it with relish, being glad of the chance to prove yourself the better man.

It is not always natural for a player to be aggressive at the start, especially if he is getting into a game with fellows bigger and more experienced than he is. But you have to school yourself to welcome such a match, because it will prepare you to tackle tough opposition. What if there is a strong chance that you will get licked? There is still a chance that you may win and you should have your eye on that chance from the minute the contest begins. Go to the plate glad of the opportunity to match your ability against the best your neighborhood can produce. There is no glory in knocking over the set-ups. Look for bigger and better competition all the time and if you don't win the first time, tell yourself you will do it next time.

But don't let aggressiveness turn into recklessness. Use your head all the time to keep from taking wild and unnecessary chances. The idea is not to exhibit your power, your strength, and your speed. It is to *win*. Sometimes that takes craft rather than power, sometimes alertness and control rather than speed.

Know the score at all times. Keep your eye always on the ball. Look for sudden opportunities and be prepared for sudden and unexpected moves by the other guy. Remember that baseball is a team game that will often require you to put aside individual glory for the sake of bringing your team in first.

Do these things and you will become a better batter and baserunner. You will also get a lot more fun out of the game.